Contents

SECURING FREEDOM

ELIZA MANNINGHAM-BULLER

P

PROFILE BOOKS

First published in Great Britain in 2012 by
PROFILE BOOKS LTD
3A Exmouth House
Pine Street
London ECIR OJH
www.profilebooks.com

A shortened version of *Securing Freedom* was broadcast on BBC
Radio 4 as the Reith Lectures 2011, entitled 'Securing Freedom'.

1 3 5 7 9 10 8 6 4 2

Printed and bound by
CPI Group (UK) Ltd, Croydon, CR0 4YY

A CIP catalogue record for this book is available from
the British Library.

ISBN 978 1 78125 015 0
eISBN 978 1 84765 851 7

The paper this book is printed on is certified by the © 1996 Forest
Stewardship Council A.C. (FSC). It is ancient-forest friendly. The
printer holds FSC chain of custody SGS-COC-2061

FSC
Mixed Sources
Product group from well-managed
forests and other controlled sources

Cert no. SGS-COC-2061
www.fsc.org
© 1996 Forest Stewardship Council

To the staff of the Security Service,
past and present.

Introduction

This book, based on the Reith Lectures which I gave in 2011 and an earlier lecture I gave in 2010, is dedicated to the staff, past and present, of the Security Service, of which I was a member for thirty-three years.

Given that their names are not known, other than to their families and their colleagues, I want to use this brief introduction to describe them. Fiction often describes intelligence officers as unscrupulous cynics, driving Ferraris (bicycles are more likely in real life), ignoring the law, obsessed by sex, alcohol and gadgets and preoccupied with internecine rivalries. Not so. My colleagues were committed and conscientious, motivated not by large salaries and bonuses but by the importance and value of their work. They often worked under great pressure, well aware of the potential consequences of the choices that they made in intelligence work. They did not expect recognition, either of their skills or their successes. When their friends in other occupations chatted about work, they became adept at turning conversations away from themselves. In their social lives they may have had to listen to people pontificating about events in the news and resist the urge to correct them. In their closest relationships they had to decide when to break cover and to whom they could safely reveal their employer. Their lives and their finances were regularly scrutinised through vetting; they surrendered some personal privacy and freedom of movement. They thought about what they were doing, the standards they needed to maintain, the ethical issues that arose. They were familiar with the law and sensitive to the society in which they worked and which they represented. They were self-critical – how could the organisation do better,

how could it learn from its mistakes?
And, like many public servants, they
learned to rise above uninformed criticism from some parts of the media.

I was proud to lead them. When I
retired in 2007, it felt a bit like bereave-
ment. I did not miss knowing secrets, the
excitement of operations, the highs and
lows, the political context. My adrenalin
flowed more sluggishly and I liked that.
What I missed were my colleagues, being
part of a trusted team of people of high
integrity, shrewd intelligence, imagina-
tion, arcane skills and determination,
who often made me laugh.

I was surprised when the BBC asked
me to give the Reith Lectures, sharing
the series with Aung San Suu Kyi. It had
never occurred to me that I might receive
such an invitation. I never saw myself,
and still don't, as an intellectual in the
tradition of Reith speakers. When I was
invited I made the mistake of looking up
the list of previous speakers, from Ber-
trand Russell onwards. This was not good

for my confidence and I doubted that I had enough worth saying to attract the scale of audience that the BBC expected. But as I came to write, to reject, to reorganise and to check on clichés, platitudes and the usual traps, I realised that there were indeed things I wished to say. And that, although I had retired from the Security Service over four years before, this was an unexpected but welcome opportunity to give my views on some important issues: freedom, security, the rule of law and intelligence.

The first three chapters of this book largely follow the Reith Lectures, while chapter four is based on a lecture I gave to an audience at the House of Lords in 2010. Chapter one discusses terrorism, ten years on from 9/11, the fear it induced and the threat to our freedom. The second chapter considers the role of security intelligence in protecting our lives and our freedom. Chapter three describes the wider policy context of these issues, both foreign and domestic.

Finally, chapter four expands on my view of intelligence and its uses.

1

Terror

On the day of the 9/11 attacks on New York and Washington, I was working in my office as usual. I was deputy head of the British Security Service and responsible for its intelligence operations. I came out of the room and my staff were standing, watching the television in silence. It was difficult quite to take in what we were seeing. But we quickly recognised that this was terrorism and came to the immediate conclusion that al-Qaeda was responsible. I am not sure whether we stopped to eat but I do know that we spent the rest of the day checking past intelligence, directing the collection of more intelligence and preparing briefings and papers for the government.

The next day I flew to Washington to talk to our American colleagues about what had happened and to offer support. With me were the head of the Secret Intelligence Service, more usually known as MI6, and the head of GCHQ, our signals intelligence agency. American airspace was closed and the officer in charge of the RAF station at Brize Norton was reluctant to let us take off, but the Prime Minister had agreed with the President that we should go. We landed at Andrews Air Force Base and drove in convoy to CIA headquarters. We found our American friends from the CIA, the FBI and NSA, the American signals intelligence agency, angry, shocked and tired but also resilient and determined. They had had no sleep. Casualty numbers were, as yet, unavailable and there were fears of an even higher death toll than was, in fact, the case. We were all haunted by images of the attack planes full of passengers, the slashes in the sides of the twin towers of the World Trade Centre, collapsing floors, the raging fires, people jumping to their deaths to escape them, pedestrians shrouded in dust and emerging tales of loss and also of heroism.

In our sobering talks with the Americans we focused on al-Qaeda, having no doubt of its responsibility for the atrocities. Bin Laden had made it clear that he wished to kill Americans and their allies and before 9/11 substantial intelligence effort had been directed against him and his group. While the actual attacks were a shock, we had been concerned all summer by intelligence of developing al-Qaeda plans. And the attacks shared characteristics which were familiar to us: coordinated suicide attacks designed to cause maximum casualties, carefully planned and executed without warning. We discussed how intelligence could be developed to provide more extensive insights to al-Qaeda to try to prevent further attacks. Obviously the United States has many more intelligence resources than the UK, but they welcomed our offer of support. And, of course, after thirty years of conflict in Northern Ireland, we had greater experience of terrorism on our own soil.

After the talks, we went back to the British Embassy. We were all in a reflective mood and in the garden we talked late into the night about what had happened and what the next steps might be. We discussed whether the United States would take direct military action in Afghanistan, where al-Qaeda was based. What were the security implications for our own citizens? We mulled on the various options open to the US Government and, more widely, to other Western governments. One of those present argued that the peace process between Israel and the Palestinians needed to be revived, an explicit recognition that the West needed to readdress the open sore in the Middle East that could well have contributed to these events. Those present agreed. It was important, even so soon after a monstrous crime, to consider all possible ways of reducing the likelihood of further attacks. Despite talk of military action, there was one thing we all agreed on: terrorism is resolved through politics and economics not through arms and intelligence, however important a role these play.

And I call it a crime, not an act of war. Terrorism is a violent tool used for political reasons to bring pressure on governments by creating fear in the populace. In the same way, I have never thought it helpful to refer to a 'war' on terror, any more than to a war on drugs. For one thing, that legitimises the terrorists as warriors; for another thing terrorism is a technique, not a state. Moreover terrorism will continue in some form whatever the outcome, if there is one, of such a 'war'. For me what happened was a crime and needs to be thought of as such. What made it different from earlier attacks was its scale and audacity, not its nature.

I understand that the United States with its long tradition of offering sanctuary to the 'huddled masses' under the towering figure of the Statue of Liberty and its belief, sometimes surprising to a European, of its land being a safe refuge, saw 9/11 as a declaration of war on its own soil, to which a military response was necessary and appropriate. But actually 9/11 was the next episode in al-Qaeda's targeting of the United States and her allies, explicitly stated by Bin Laden as his intention and already demonstrated, for example, by the attacks on the US Embassies in Dar es Salaam and Nairobi in 1998 and on the USS Cole in the Yemen in 2000.

My colleagues and I, and our friends around the world, had often tried to second guess what terrorist groups might do next. Sometimes we were steered by intelligence and were able to take precautions. But we also tried to think laterally about what we, if motivated by the convictions of a terrorist, might do to inflict major damage on a nation and to instill fear in its citizens. Terrorist groups learn and change. The Provisional IRA had moved from killing and maiming drinkers in crowded Birmingham pubs to its more sophisticated attacks on the City of London, which were designed to drive away foreign investment and hurt the UK economically. I think what shocked us all on 9/11 was the realisation that these events changed the world, that, if terrorists could successfully mount such attacks within the United States, anything was possible.

Bin Laden must have expected that these murderous attacks would force a reaction that would make it easier for him to persuade others of his argument that Islam was under attack from the West. It suited his agenda for Muslims to be viewed with suspicion. In addition to mass casualties, Bin Laden sought an economic impact through driving up security costs and disrupting normal life. Our imaginations, spurred by these events and by intelligence, took rein on what else al-Qaeda might do. The prospect of chemical, bacteriological or radiological terrorism looked more likely. Bin Laden had said in 1998 that acquiring chemical or nuclear weapons to defend Muslims was a 'religious duty' and that was a very real concern in the years afterwards. We knew, and know now, how fragile our security can be. The extreme stories of fiction and film no longer seemed so fantastic, although much of what we argued and worried about has not happened, not least because of the efforts internationally of security and intelligence agencies and the police.

Was it an attack on freedom itself as some have asserted? I think the answer is complex. In her Reith Lecture in 2011, Aung San Suu Kyi talked of the right to live 'free from fear'. She was speaking in the context of living under a cruel and capricious military junta, and we all hope that her patient opposition to it will succeed. But there are also threats to our freedoms in the democracies of the

West. We expect to live largely free from fear, at least the fear of being blown to bits when going about our daily lives. So there was an attack on that freedom. We were all alarmed. For example, I remember how, for months, whenever I heard a plane overhead I looked up and wondered if it was on course and being flown by bona fide pilots.

There are a few Muslims who argue that democracy – the right to elect a secular government – does not accord with Islamic principles. A bit of history here. Sayyid Qutb, a leading member of the Muslim Brotherhood in Egypt, was disgusted by what he thought was the immorality and materialism of the United States when he lived there as a student shortly after the Second World War. That view influenced his disciple, al-Zawahiri, now the leader of al-Qaeda. Both could be said to have disliked the freedom of American citizens to live as they wish within the law. It is perhaps worth noting that the modern Muslim

Brotherhood does not subscribe to those non-democratic views and actually condemned 9/11.

But I still find it difficult to accept that the terror attacks were on 'freedom' or democracy as some have claimed. The young men who committed the crime came from countries without democratic rights and freedoms, with no liberty to express their views in open debate, no easy way of changing their rulers, no opportunity for choice and well aware that the West often supported those autocratic rulers. For them, as for many others, an external enemy was, I believe, a unifying way of addressing some of their own frustrations.

Of course some recruits to al-Qaeda have enjoyed the freedom of living in the West, the right to vote, to speak out, to engage in political debate. They have in many cases received subsidised further education, free health care and lived with considerable material possessions. They have enjoyed human rights and freedom under the law. So what unites them with the unenfranchised and unfree end of the terrorist spectrum? It is the view, exemplified by the Palestinians' plight, but not only that, that the oil-hungry West has exploited and occupied Muslim lands, supported dictators and killed their citizens. The Crusades are not forgotten. And we believe that it was the arrival of American bases in the holy lands of Saudi Arabia that first motivated Osama Bin Laden to attack the West, especially the USA, and to launch a global jihad. Indeed the three stated aims of al-Qaeda are to remove the United States and its allies from the Arab lands, to depose apostate rulers and to restore the Islamic form of government known as the caliphate.

It would be wrong to suggest that all terrorists connected to al-Qaeda or its affiliates share an identical motivation. Yet a single narrative, compelling to some, does seem to prevail: that it is the duty of good Muslims to wage jihad against the West, to avenge their Palestinian co-religionists, and more recently those in Iraq, Afghanistan and elsewhere. If you watch the chilling video wills made by the British 7/7 bombers, or those convicted in London for the ambitious plot of 2006 to destroy a series of transatlantic aircraft to mark the fifth anniversary of 9/11, it is clear that their perception of revenge is the main motive.

Moreover, for some, including some third-generation Britons, the prospect of engagement with al-Qaeda offers a sense of identity and a focus which they mistakenly think is noble in a society they may find alien. I am convinced that many are not driven by the al-Qaeda ideology but by the attraction of belonging to a group which does something exciting and gives a purpose to their lives. Loyalty to the group then becomes the main motivation. And, of course, those committed to the cause are unscrupulous about exploiting and grooming young and vulnerable people for terrorist acts.

When we flew back to the United Kingdom, two days after 9/11, up the eastern seaboard of the United States, the smoke from the fires in New York was clearly visible. We felt alone in the skies above America. On the long flight home we discussed the likelihood of further attacks and what could be done to prevent them, and how the United States and the rest of the world would react. The sympathy with what America had suffered was profound and widespread. The majority of nations offered their solidarity and support. There had been a graphic and appalling illustration of what a few determined individuals could achieve to bring terror not only to North America but also beyond. America felt vulnerable. We all did. Airline bookings dropped as capital cities were avoided and holidays cancelled. For the United Kingdom and my Service, what followed was a time of great anxiety and tension, as floods of information reached us.

Was a copy-cat attack to be launched on Canary Wharf? How should the government deal with an incoming passenger aircraft known to be under terrorist control, or, worse in terms of decision making, suspected of so being? Where would al-Qaeda hit next? What defences could we strengthen? What could we do to reduce apprehension and to encourage our citizens to continue their lives, as far as possible free from fear? What could we anticipate? Which of the flood of leads should we pursue? Which put to one side? That presented us with tough choices. We could not pursue everything yet knew that what we neglected could develop into a potent threat. Research was in hand to revisit old leads and to reinterpret old information in the light of these new events.

But, looking back, I think that those of us working in intelligence and security were privileged. We had a clear task and we were extremely focused. We did not share that feeling of impotence which terrorism can bring to people. We knew what we all had to do: to strengthen our intelligence effort in an attempt to anticipate and pre-empt the terrorists. My concern was that staff would exhaust themselves, so driven was everyone by their understanding of the immediacy of the threat.

One of the first things we did was to convene in London a meeting of heads, or their representatives, of European security services, all well known to us, and close colleagues. A senior US intelligence official travelled to London to brief us and our European friends on the discoveries from the investigation. This meeting, while unusual given its horrific backdrop, was not unique. Security and intelligence services regularly meet to exchange views, share concerns and work together. The Americans, whose intelligence collection efforts dwarf most others, are generous. Sharing intelligence is not always straightforward because of differing approaches and legal frameworks, but at that meeting we were all among friends whom we trusted. Most of those present had had their own experiences of terrorism and later had further manifestations of al-Qaeda-related terror to deal with. We in the United Kingdom had had to deal with Palestinian, Syrian, Libyan, Moroccan and Algerian terrorists, to name but a few. Our most significant experience was, of course, with terrorism stemming from Ireland.

That had preoccupied us for years. Some of the things we learned are relevant to thinking about the very different threat from al-Qaeda. One is the belief that the divisions in Northern Irish society, manifested in terrorism, could not be solved militarily. Nor could intelligence and police work, however successful in preventing attacks and informing governments, resolve those divisions, although that work could buy time for a political process. Intelligence was critical in helping ministers manage that process, the aim of which was to reach long-term political resolutions with those who had prosecuted the terrorist campaign. But it took many years and extraordinary commitment by politicians, especially the Prime Minister, Tony Blair, and the Irish Taoiseach, Bertie Ahern, to reach that point. And peace only came, at least largely peace, when the two ends of the political spectrum, Sinn Fein and the Democratic Unionist Party, reached agreement.

In the garden of the British Embassy in Washington on the day after 9/11, we discussed the near certainty of a war in Afghanistan to destroy the al-Qaeda bases there and drive out the terrorists and their sponsors, the Taliban. We all saw that as necessary. And in Afghanistan documents and rudimentary laboratories were discovered showing the terrorists' keen interest in fulfilling Bin Laden's stricture to acquire and use nuclear material. What I think none of us anticipated at that stage was that the unity of purpose directed at preventing further success by al-Qaeda would be tested by the decision of the United States, supported by the UK and others, to invade Iraq and remove Saddam Hussein, after the rout of the Taliban in Afghanistan. Saddam Hussein certainly allowed no freedom. His human rights record was atrocious and his prisons torture chambers. He was a ruthless dictator and the world is better off without him. But neither he nor his regime had anything to do with 9/11 and despite an extensive search for links, none but the most trivial and insignificant was found. Indeed, for the secular Saddam Hussein, al-Qaeda represented a challenge to his authority.

The invasion of Iraq polarised international opinion. Many doubted its legality. War was declared on a rogue state, an easier target than an elusive terrorist group based mainly, at that stage, in the difficult terrain of the Afghan-Pakistani border, and, in my view, whatever the merits of putting an end to Saddam Hussein, the war was also a distraction from the pursuit of al-Qaeda. It increased the terrorist threat by convincing more people that Osama Bin Laden's claim that Islam was under attack was correct. It provided an arena for the jihad for which he had called, so that many of his supporters, including British citizens, travelled to Iraq to attack Western forces. It also showed very clearly that foreign and domestic policy are intertwined – actions overseas have an impact at home. Without doubt our involvement in Iraq spurred some young British Muslims to turn to terror.

Nine eleven was a cruel crime on a vast scale. It propelled Bin Laden and his supporters into the consciousness of the whole world. It altered our perception of what terrorism could achieve. It led to the recruitment of like-minded terrorists across the globe from Spain to Indonesia, from Kenya to Canada, from Pakistan to the Netherlands. It led to massive expenditure by the West as it sought to defend itself. And what now? Eighteen months ago, I predicted that the so-called 'war on terror' would not be won but that the threat would mutate and might moderate. I note that the threat level in the United Kingdom and to British interests abroad was lowered earlier in the summer. It is probably too soon to be able to judge with any confidence the effect of Bin Laden's death. But I do not expect terrorism as a tool, often used by states in earlier decades, now used largely by groups, to disappear. And I very much doubt that my former colleagues are relaxed about the continuing threat from al-Qaeda and its sympathisers.

The Northern Ireland example, so utterly different as it is, and even with the recent worrying upsurge in dissident terrorist activity, should encourage us to hope that peace between hostile factions is possible. Who could have thought – I certainly didn't – that we would see Ian

Paisley and Martin McGuinness, Chief Minister and Deputy Minister respectively, laughing together on a sofa while promoting trade in North America? And maybe, just maybe, the death of Bin Laden, the excitement of the Arab Spring, the possibility of a new and more enlightened generation of Muslim leaders, will mean that we see less al-Qaeda-related terrorism. There are some causes for optimism, including the attrition the terrorists have suffered, the changing politics of the Middle East and the investment in intelligence and its successes. This last will be the subject of chapter two. I am also encouraged that most people refuse to give the victory to the terrorists either by being intimidated or by supporting the diminution of our civil liberties. Ten years on from 9/11, the fear that afflicted us then has faded, although it has certainly not disappeared.

Security

For thirty-three years of my life I was a member of the British Security Service, popularly known as MI5. When I joined in 1974, recruitment was a bit haphazard. I met someone at a party and with the minimum of effort, found myself, somewhat to my surprise, in the Service. I really had no idea what I was getting into, but I stayed for over half my life, because I enjoyed the work and its challenges. There were, of course, disappointments and setbacks but it was a privilege to work with highly motivated colleagues on a common purpose. And, when we had success, not always visible to the public, it was a great feeling.

The Service's remit, although not enshrined in law till late in its history, when it was already eighty years old, is to protect the United Kingdom from threats including terrorism, espionage and sabotage. And to protect, explicitly, parliamentary democracy. Security should not damage our most important civil liberties. It is not an accident that the Service's crest incorporates a portcullis, the symbol of the British parliament. I am often asked to speak at conferences and in debates on the theme of security versus liberty. I always refuse because I do not see these as opposites. They are different but there is no liberty without security. I wish to argue for liberty, not be falsely characterised as its opponent. The first human right listed in the European Convention of Human Rights is the right to life, the third the right to liberty and security. And the rights enshrined in the American Declaration of Independence are 'life, liberty and the pursuit of happiness.' Life surely has to include safety from being a random target of terrorism.

Security is about people being able to go about their daily lives, travelling, working, enjoying themselves without being killed or mutilated. There is, of course, no such thing as 100 per cent security. Life is full of risks and no government can guarantee its citizens' safety and should never suggest that it can. But we, in the UK and in the West, have an expectation of not having to live under a cloud of fear from terrorist attack. We also assume that we can speak our minds, throw out our governments, live under the rule of law with an independent judiciary and an accountable police service and we expect high standards from officials paid out of the public purse. We enjoy our civil liberties. We should not fear arbitrary arrest and, if we are accused of having broken the law, we expect proper and fair legal process.

So a key role of Britain's Security Service is to protect parliamentary democracy. In the past, that has involved extensive work against totalitarian, communist and fascist regimes and their supporters. Today we may, complacently perhaps, assume that those ideologies, with their lack of freedom, are discredited and unlikely to gain strength again. But in the twentieth century they offered serious threats to our democracy. The imaginative and courageous work against fascism in the Second World War is well-documented. Intelligence and security work – such as the operations designed to deceive Germany about the D-Day landings and the breaking of the German codes – played an important part in the defeat of Nazi Germany. Similarly, in the Cold War, crucial work was done to limit Soviet influence. When we look back on the Cold War, we wonder at the massive cost of it, the distorted perspectives and the mutual misunderstanding. At the time however, we felt threatened by a heavily-armed totalitarian regime, an 'evil empire' indeed, which had colonised most of its neighbours by force and whose citizens enjoyed none of the freedoms or rights that we enjoy. Like the Nazis, with whom they had a non-aggression pact for the first two years of the Second World War, the Soviets killed vast numbers of their own citizens and governed through fear.

So why do we need organisations such as the one I feel privileged to have been a member of for over half my life? I think the answer is simple. While some threats to us are obvious, some of the most dangerous are not. In order to expose and counter such threats a state needs to acquire intelligence about them. Intelligence is information that is deliberately intended to be concealed. To quote Lord Butler's review of intelligence on weapons of mass destruction in Iraq, 'much ingenuity and effort is spent making secret information difficult to acquire and hard to analyse.' To obtain it we have to use covert methods. We have to read, listen, look and follow secretly. We have to approach people and ask them to provide information in confidence. Those human sources who agree to provide such information usually do so for brave and principled reasons. I have met people willing to risk their own lives to save others, or jeopardise their own freedom so that others may be free. They are unlikely ever to receive public recognition for the good they do. The most moving and humbling experiences of my career have been meeting such people. We all have cause to be tremendously grateful to them.

Now, I was brought up to value privacy and respect it. I was taught not to eavesdrop on others' conversations or to read their letters. The European Convention on Human Rights lists in Article Eight the right to a private life. However it acknowledges a few exceptions when that right is trumped, for example by the need for national security. It felt uncomfortable – I think I was naïve – when I joined the Service to discover that the state intruded into the privacy of a few of its citizens and some of those of foreign states. But I came to see that such intrusion was justified, and could only be justified, if the threat it sought to counter by such intrusion was serious. It was about necessity and proportion. Eavesdropping on plans to threaten our freedoms and our lives was a route to protecting them. It was necessary to intrude into the privacy of a few so that the majority could be safer.

What I came to appreciate was the necessity of such intrusions being properly authorised by the law. When I joined the Service there was no legislation to cover its work. We argued for security intelligence work to be properly recognised in law. The Security Service Act of 1989 was long overdue. The government of Mrs Thatcher was not, at first, convinced of its necessity, but its importance was critical. The Service's experience of working on a proper legislative basis has been wholly positive. Even at that early stage, in 1989, we knew its significance.

When the Cold War ended, the emerging democracies of Eastern Europe, who were considering how best to protect their freedom, sought the advice of services like mine. Their experience of security and intelligence agencies were as repressive organs of state control, at best. Having suffered under the Gestapo, in many cases, as well as the KGB, they saw that they needed properly-constituted new security and intelligence agencies to protect their freedom. We emphasised that their agencies needed a proper legal foundation and they took our advice. In South Africa, too, after Mandela came to power, I remember discussing with the new ANC government how to legislate for security and intelligence agencies. I was especially struck by seeing an ANC official, in exile all his life, working alongside a white colleague from the old service. He said to me 'his father tortured mine,' but they were working together to create a service which could protect the new South Africa.

For many around the world, including Aung San Suu Kyi and her Burmese colleagues, the security services are in effect state-controlled terrorists, instilling fear in their people through violence or the threat of it. But in a democracy, a properly-constituted and overseen security service accountable to the law and with a legislative base, is, I believe, essential. In some democratic countries the functions fall to the police rather than to a separate civilian service as in the UK. I prefer our system where the Security Service has no powers of arrest or detention.

And, of course, intelligence can help in many ways. I have mentioned its strategic importance in the Second World War. It has also saved many lives in peacetime and contributed to the development of policy. How else could our government judge that the time was ripe to talk to the Provisional IRA? How else to understand and protest at the behaviour of the man described as 'the father' of the Pakistani bomb, AQ Khan, who sold nuclear technology to Iran, Libya and other countries, including the criminal state of North Korea, whose people are again eating grass? How else to prevent the terrorist attack, planned for the fifth anniversary of 9/11, which, if successful, would have blown out of the air up to a dozen transatlantic aircraft, with a projected death toll exceeding even 9/11? For intelligence doesn't only constrain terrorist violence; it also helps governments to understand the ideas, the aspirations and the relationships that characterise the terrorists and their supporters. It may also be factored in to the development of foreign and domestic policy, but should not be the basis of it.

Intelligence work presents some complex ethical issues, well beyond the level of my parents' strictures not to listen to others' telephone calls or read their letters. As I have said, intrusion into privacy must be necessary and proportionate to the threat it aims to counter. What is proportionate and who decides? Those are crunch questions. The important constitutional principle, enshrined in law, is that the operations of the Security Service are the responsibility of the Director General who reports to the Home Secretary. The government can not direct whom the Service investigates. This is an important safeguard against the politicisation of the Service's work. But the government *can* stop the Service deploying its more intrusive techniques, intercepting communications between people or eavesdropping on their private conversations by microphone.

These techniques have to be authorised in advance, in law, by a Secretary of State, usually the Home Secretary, who decides whether he or she agrees with the Service that the case for a warrant is strong enough to justify it. Warrants that are issued are later scrutinised by specially appointed commissioners, former senior judges, for legality and proportionality, and they report each year to the Prime Minister with the non-secret parts of their reports being laid before Parliament. The Parliamentary Intelligence and Security Committee, which my Service argued for, continues to evolve its scrutiny. Because it meets in private, as it must, it is underestimated by those who seek a transparent process. Ultimately the Service is answerable to the law and the courts.

I recognise that my answer as to who decides what is proportionate will not satisfy the sceptical, but, during my time in the Service, I found it sensitive about its work, with a properly narrow perspective on what it should be engaged in. At various stages in its history, for example, the Service has elected to be deaf to the suggestion by government that it should study legitimate organisations – such as the Campaign for Nuclear Disarmament. We respected the law, argued for accountability when we did not have it and fostered a culture of rigorous, sceptical, objective assessment and judgement. If you went into Thames House, the Security Service headquarters, you would find a largely young workforce

of men and women from diverse back-
grounds, with professional intelligence
skills who, in my view rightly, believe
that they are doing an important and
valuable job. They are amused by the fic-
tional presentation of what they do. The
Service to which they belong will not get
everything right, no organisation does,
but it tries to acknowledge and learn
from its mistakes.

So how, in a globalised world, with an
international threat, should we work?
I mentioned in chapter one the close
co-operation between intelligence and
security services in Europe and with the
United States, who are generous provid-
ers of intelligence which has contributed
significantly to our safety. We need to
understand what is happening outside the
UK as well as in it; al-Qaeda has extensive tentacles and many terrorist plots
here have had overseas links. How can
we work safely with foreign services who
may have no democratic accountability
and who operate in ways which would

clearly be illegal in the UK? With caution and sometimes with great difficulty, as events in Libya have clearly illustrated. We have to make judgements which balance the greater good against some of the evils that men do. No one could justify what went on under Gaddafi's regime, but awkward relationships are sometimes preferable to the alternative dangers of isolation and mutual enmity.

The allegations about possible extraordinary rendition to Libya and the intelligence documents disclosed in Tripoli in 2011 raised widespread concern that the judgements with regard to Libya were wrong. These issues are now the subject of a police investigation to see whether any crimes have been committed and are therefore now sub judice.

Torture is illegal in our national law and in international law. It is wrong and never justified. It is a sadness, and worse, that the previous government of our great ally, the United States, chose to waterboard some detainees. The argument that life-saving intelligence was thereby obtained, and I accept it was, still does not justify it. Torture should be utterly rejected even when it may offer the prospect of saving lives. I am proud my Service refused to turn to the torture of high-level German prisoners in the Second World War, when, in the early years, we stood alone and there was a high risk of our being invaded and becoming a Nazi province. So if not then, why should it be justified now?

I believe that the acquisition of short-term gain through waterboarding and other forms of mistreatment was a profound mistake and lost the United States moral authority and some of the widespread sympathy it had enjoyed as a result of 9/11. I am confident that I know the answer to the question of whether torture has made the world a safer place. It hasn't.

In chapter one I referred to the wealth of intelligence that flowed after 9/11 as security and intelligence agencies around the world worked desperately to prevent the next attack. In the UK we felt inundated and almost swamped with leads to plots, by the plethora of incomplete intelligence, sometimes fragmentary, sometimes false, often contradictory, to be analysed, assessed and developed until action could be taken. The pressure was acute, the concern of the government and the public palpable. Britain was clearly a target, as was horribly illustrated by the attacks on the British consulate and on HSBC bank headquarters in Turkey in 2003. And British nationals, who had been based and possibly trained in Afghanistan, were a major concern. People here in the UK described as 'home-grown' were of concern well before 7/7. Richard Reid, the first, but not the only, shoe-bomber, who tried to bring down an aircraft only months after 9/11, was British and converted to terrorism here. Staff in all the British services, my own, MI6, GCHQ and the police, were very stretched.

No sooner had we resolved one plot than several more emerged. Indeed they proliferated, partly because of our involvement in Iraq. We had to juggle resources and make excruciating choices on what to pursue. Excessive hours were worked as we struggled to understand the scale of what we were facing. The government agreed to an unprecedented doubling of our budget, but it took some time to build up the organisation as we trained new recruits. We opened eight new regional offices, scrutinised and improved our recruitment, training, IT, intelligence methods, analytical techniques and data collection. We also proposed a new cross-departmental terrorism assessment group, now the Joint Terrorist Analysis Centre. During the time I was Director General, our committed staff, supported by colleagues from MI6, GCHQ, other departments and the police, increased the number of intelligence operations fivefold.

So was the taxpayers' investment

worth it? Others must judge, but I note that from 9/11 until I retired in 2007, we faced fifteen serious terrorist plots and many, many smaller ones. The plots were of varying complexity and sophistication and most involved a network of people overseas as well as people based in the UK. We detected and thwarted, with the police, a dozen of them, not a mean achievement. Three were undetected in advance: 7/7, 21/7 and Richard Reid. Richard Reid was prevented by an alert air stewardess from detonating his shoe bomb. The bombs of the four men responsible for the attempted attacks on 21/7 failed to explode and they were all arrested within eight days. Only the four suicide bombers of 7/7 succeeded, causing the deaths of fifty-two innocent commuters, with many more seriously injured and maimed.

I can be grateful that we were able to protect life and prevent terror through countless operations including the most ambitious, the airline plot, planned as a spectacular terrorist attack to mark the fifth anniversary of 9/11. But I shall never forget the human tragedy of 7/7. As with 9/11, the images will not fade: the mangled bus; the victim whose burned face was covered by a paper mask; the grainy film of the bombers, both on their reconnaissance and on the final, fateful day; the dignity of the bereaved at the inquest. I wish so much that it had been possible to stop it, but the Service expects to be judged by what we did not prevent, not what we did. It was a grim day and I can vividly recall the sickening feeling when we thought we had a repeat on 21/7. I can remember my acute apprehension that this might be a pattern and that the resilience and determination of Londoners not to be cowed and to come to work as usual might be gradually eroded and that fear might prevail.

The Security Service has always believed that the best result of a counter-terrorist operation is a successful prosecution. We live under the rule of law and are grateful for that. Prosecution can cause difficulties but they can generally be overcome.

The first difficulty is the decision, the responsibility of the police, on when to arrest. Too soon, the evidence is inadequate, no one can be charged and there will be media criticism. Too late and the attack has occurred and the authorities are severely criticised for foreknowledge.

Secondly, not all intelligence can be turned into evidence. It can fall well short. The Service must deal with hearsay at third hand, things said, things overheard, things which are open to varying interpretation even with the benefit of hindsight. Some of this intelligence is designed to mislead, all of it needs validation, analysis and assessment and would be kicked out by a judge even if the prosecution thought it useable. To protect public safety, the police often need to disrupt plots on the basis of intelligence but before evidence sufficient to bring criminal charges has been collected. That requires us to accept that not everyone who presents a threat can be prosecuted.

And thirdly, sources of intelligence are fragile. Individuals who supply it often risk torture and death. They put their trust in us. Our duty is to protect them and their human rights. Techniques can be compromised and become unusable. If we compromise intelligence sources and risk the lives of those who bravely give us information, we shall soon have no intelligence and the risks to our lives and our liberty will rocket. Those who argue for a world without secrets would be less safe if their wishes were met. But, and this is an important but, we must still seek prosecutions as we do not resort to offshore internment as the Bush administration did. I am proud that some 240 individuals have been subject to proper legal process and convicted of terrorist-related offences since 9/11. That is the way to deal with terrorist crime. But for long-term success and a reduction in the threat, politics and especially foreign policy, have to play their crucial parts. And that will be the subject of chapter three.

3

Freedom

Chapter one discussed terrorism ten years on from 9/11 and its implications for our freedom. Chapter two considered the ways in which security intelligence protects our lives and our freedom. Now I want to consider the wider policy context. I do not do so as an expert in foreign or domestic policy, but as a retired security intelligence officer.

I want to argue that states should, wherever possible, seek political solutions and reconciliation. Secondly, that how a nation conducts its foreign policy has a direct bearing on its chances of success in the search for conciliation. And finally, I want to consider how our handling of risk, and the laws we pass to deal with it, can distort our response to the threat of terrorism.

In al-Qaeda we see a terrorist grouping

with, in many ways, a medieval ideology, employing today's technology to great advantage. It works in a thoroughly modern way, virtual, amorphous, franchised and unbounded by geography. It has recruited people from all over the world. It understands the power of images, both in its campaign of terror and in its recruitment and proselytising material. It skillfully exploits the instant communications and social networking of the IT age. I think it also understands some of the vulnerability of the West: its appetite for news, its short-termism, its instant judgements and the pressures on its governments to respond to terrorism and the limited options open to them.

When I joined the Security Service, there was no internet, international travel was expensive, there was less migration, borders were not generally porous and communications were usually by a fixed line telephone or a letter. I can remember special kettles being kept for steaming open letters. That will no longer suffice.

The democratic state can no longer rely on its old tools to collect the intelligence it needs to protect itself. It will always wish to recruit human sources to provide inside information, but it also needs, subject to proper controls, oversight and legal safeguards, to try to redress the balance by using the latest powerful technologies to react quickly and keep it one step ahead. The terrorist now has at his disposal tools which were once the sole preserve of the state. He has more advanced means of conspiring, mobilising and causing death and damage. So what it is ethical, necessary and proportionate for the state to do in response cannot be set in stone.

I have known throughout my career that, however professional security and intelligence agencies working with the police may be and whatever success they may have in preventing terrorist crimes, they cannot stop everything. Similarly, however resourceful the terrorists may be, they will suffer attrition, betrayal, arrest, imprisonment, as well as death.

Success for us will not be the absence of terror but less of it, with fewer deaths and a dwindling supply of new recruits. That success is not likely to come from military effort or from security, intelligence and police work alone, but from long-term political and economic initiatives aimed at reducing the causes of terrorism and countering extreme ideology in order to seek the peace and reconciliation that has been so striking in South Africa. Conciliation is never easy, sometimes impossible, but it is always worth trying. Security and intelligence work can play a valuable role in creating space for the political process which is central to that, but it cannot replace it.

So what might these political initiatives be? Some of the answers may be found in the Arab Spring. Last year, triggered by the self-immolation of a Tunisian street trader, we have seen people in North Africa and the Middle East take to the streets and sometimes to arms in protest at the conditions under which they live. The list is long: Tunisia, Algeria, Lebanon, Jordan, Sudan, Oman, Saudi Arabia, Egypt, Syria, Morocco, Yemen, Bahrain, Kuwait and, of course, Libya.

Conditions in these countries obviously vary but what the protesters have in common is most simply stated by a leader of the Syrian protests: 'We want what you have – freedom.' They are protesting in many cases at venal dictators, at absolute monarchs, at lack of human rights, at lack of freedom and association. They also, of course, want jobs, houses and education and some share of the material wealth, which, where it exists, is too often monopolised by their rulers. Their passion for freedom shines out, encouraged by the visibility offered by the internet and promoted by social networks. They are prepared to risk their lives for the freedom we enjoy.

The Arab Spring raises serious questions about al-Qaeda's relevance. It has not been able to respond convincingly to the widespread demand for change, despite its adroit use of technology and the media. Al-Qaeda's version of the ideal Islamic government seems to have had little appeal. The Arab Spring also conclusively shows the hollowness of the cynical comments I have too often heard, that people elsewhere do not want democracy and, with no tradition of it, would not know how to practice it. There were similar patronising comments made about the countries of Eastern Europe when the Soviet Empire broke up and the Berlin Wall came down. There is also, among some, an assumption that any government replacing a dictatorship will become corrupt and unstable, subject to malign influences. But the fact that democracy often has a tough birth means that we should offer support where that is practical.

Our foreign policy must never forget that desire for freedom. It must encourage it, both to meet the wishes of those who lack it and for our own long-term self-interest. Perhaps inevitably short-term interests will intrude. Every now and again, governments assert the need for an ethical foreign policy. That laudable aim usually bumps up against the reality that many countries of the world are led by unscrupulous autocrats who use every means to hold on to power. They have little concern for the people they govern and often maintain power only by imprisoning their opponents and bribing their armed forces. Several of these countries are vital to our economic and security interests. Unfortunately there is no point talking only to our friends and allies. The world is a messy place and we need to engage with the people in power.

From my own perspective in the Security Service, I know that protecting British citizens would be impossible if we were restricted to talking to those whose values we share. I can remember plots to attack us, for example, with links to Indonesia, Somalia, the Philippines,

Kenya, Algeria, Jordan and, of course, most importantly, Pakistan. That list is not comprehensive. We cannot just talk to the Swiss, however enjoyable and easy that might be.

So what then of the contentious rapprochement with Gaddafi in 2003? I do not think that it was wrong in principle. The prize was his abandonment of his programme for nuclear and chemical weapons. Gaddafi is the man, as I know from personal experience, who supplied explosives, arms and cash to the Provisional IRA, indirectly causing the deaths of many of the victims of Irish terrorism, as well as being responsible himself for a whole series of atrocities. They included the murder of the London police officer Yvonne Fletcher and, notably, Lockerbie.

That small Scottish town was somewhere I lived for several weeks, as we and the police tried to piece together what had happened and start the search to find the culprits. The people of Lockerbie provided us with generous helpings of home-made food as we began the slow and painful investigation to understand why and how 270 people, mainly American students flying home for Christmas, had met their death and to work towards a prosecution of those responsible. I can still see the ashen faces of young service personnel and police officers as they returned to the school, the temporary police headquarters, after long days searching for body parts and wreckage strewn over a vast area.

Gaddafi's was a brutal regime and his own people suffered most of all. Nevertheless in 2003 the Government made the difficult, but, I think, right decision to open talks. Had Gaddafi made progress with his nuclear and other programmes, he could still be in power and threatening us today. There are clearly questions to be answered about the various relationships that developed afterwards and whether the UK supped with a sufficiently long spoon.

It is right to use all our diplomatic

efforts to encourage dictators to grant their people freedom. Participation in government, the belief that people's lives can be improved and their rights protected, that you can have some say, however slight, in how you are governed, reduces the need for terrorism. Look at Northern Ireland, where former terrorists are in government. We should welcome this, not damn it. Look at many of our former colonies, whose first leaders had been imprisoned by us for terrorism. Look at Mandela and the ANC which used terror tactics when it was in exile.

In Northern Ireland, the Provisional IRA decided, partly as a result of intelligence successes against them, that pursuing a parallel policy of terrorism and politics, the Armalite and the ballot box, was outdated and it dropped the gun. The gradual move from terrorism into government is a long-established pattern. As I mentioned in chapter one, I hope that the greater freedom which should flow from the Arab Spring will undermine the attraction of the al-Qaeda narrative. If you are able to engage in your own political process, you have less cause to attack what across the Arab world is often called the 'Great Satan'.

Dialogue, not only with the dictators of the world but with the terrorists, is necessary. As Churchill said in the White House in 1954, 'to jaw-jaw is always better than to war-war.' Intelligence plays an important part and is of most value if working as part of a wider dialogue involving politics, diplomacy and economic process. My most relevant experience of this is the complex and prolonged talks in Northern Ireland. There are plenty of other examples, including talking to Hezbollah and to Hamas.

Talking doesn't mean approval. It means an attempt to reduce the threat by addressing, if possible, its causes. It is a way of exploring peaceful options, of probing possibilities, of identifying whether there is room to manoeuvre and what compromises, if any, may be reached, what political grievances can be acknowledged or even, in rare cases, accommodated. It is also the opportunity for governments to express their own positions. It requires courage by governments and a willingness to embark on an uncertain and tricky course which may well prove fruitless.

Not all terrorists are evil although their acts are. Nor are they all pathologically violent. A few are but many are not and have their own rationale, not ours, for what they do. In 1994 it was clear that the Provisional IRA was ready to move to proper talks with the British government about the future of Northern Ireland, but, misguidedly, they wished to do so from what they saw as a position of strength. So shortly before talks were due to start, they dispatched to England a vast bomb concealed in the flat bed of a lorry. It was intercepted and defused, but had it exploded, say in the centre of London, it would have been politically impossible for the government to enter talks and the peace process would have been further delayed. The Provisional IRA and its political wing, Sinn Fein, learned greater political sophistication through subsequent engagement.

And what about al-Qaeda? How might we talk to it? And do we even need to? It is not yet clear whether the death of Bin Laden has made the world a safer place and whether al-Qaeda has been permanently weakened. The Americans believe, and I obviously have no inside knowledge, that he remained the substantive leader of a dispersed organisation, the spider at the middle of the web and that his death will reduce the amount of al-Qaeda terrorism we see. I hope they may be right, but webs are resilient and I doubt that his death will be a fatal blow to the organisation he founded, or to the ideology he helped to create.

So what is there to discuss, what to negotiate about, what to agree on? Would any concessions be feasible? I don't know the answers to these questions, but I very much hope that there are those in the West who are exploring them. We are, after all, talking to the Taliban, their old sponsors and could make progress. Perhaps we should be encouraged by the recent first steps toward the establishment of a Taliban office in Qatar.

Al-Qaeda is not a disciplined organisation with a clear structure. There will be those in al-Qaeda, or associated with its franchises, who are tired and disenchanted, for whom the violence has become sterile and sickening. Some, thwarted by lack of success, will be looking for a way out. There are already those prepared to help the West. Bearing in mind that we are judged by our deeds, we should also be capable of countering the credibility of the al-Qaeda narrative, that Islam is under attack from the West.

So we should try to reduce terrorism by talking to its advocates and practitioners and try to promote freedom through talking to dictators. But we should never

forget who and what they are. We need
to avoid helping dictators to survive.
The West's record on that is poor. We
have too often preferred the stability of
the devil we know to the uncertainties
of democracy. We cannot expect people round the world to fail to notice our
hypocrisy if a gap exists between our
professed support for freedom and our
actions. People suffering from oppressive
governments are bemused when the West
talks of freedom and democracy while at
the same time supporting regimes that
deny them. Of course there may often be
much going on behind the scenes and it
is important to recognise the real value
of quiet diplomacy and private pressure
away from the glare of public criticism.

If we ourselves are to be free, and to
feel secure in our freedom, it is important to keep a rational perspective on terrorist risk. Bin Laden must have known
that 9/11 would make this especially difficult, for at least two reasons: the end-
less images of the horror, recycled and

replayed round the clock by the twenty-four hour media, and the prevalence of the unrealistic view that society can become risk free. The world is full of risks and dangers, only some of which can be reduced. There are of course reasons why people fear terrorism more acutely than other dangers. The threat of violent death is potent. It can create community tension, including irrational Islamophobia, and cause loss of confidence in government, as in Spain after the train bombings in Madrid in 2004. It also places on government the tough dilemma of providing an authoritative response without giving the terrorists the status they seek.

One of the fears since 9/11 is that it, or something similar, could happen again. And of course it still could, although I would hope that the substantial investment in security and intelligence in the last ten years has made it less likely. It nearly happened with the plot to bring down up to a dozen transatlantic aircraft

in 2006 to mark the anniversary of 9/11.
Had that occurred, the death toll would
have been very high, the economic cost
enormous and the long-term effect
frightening.

I mentioned in chapter two that,
although it is a government's responsibility to do what it can to protect its citizens
from threats, governments should never
imply that they are able to do so fully.
Politicians lose their way if they become
too apprehensive about how the media
will react to terrorism when it happens.
It is very difficult for governments to
manage both economies that are shaken
by terrorism and anxious public opinion. And there are no military or security
options that are certain of success.

And not all security risks, such as that
from a xenophobic, right-wing Norwe-
gian who appears to have acted alone, can
be anticipated and countered. Moreover,
political and media pressure to 'do something' in response to such events can lead
to unnecessary, even counterproductive,

initiatives and new laws which may offer false assurance that they will prevent the recurrence of the event which triggered them.

This is not a new phenomenon. When the Security Service was focused on Irish-related terrorism, it became used to being asked for suggestions for new legislation. There have been times when the Service has argued strongly for legislation, for example for that governing its functions and its powers. But it has rarely argued for substantial counter-terrorist powers, believing the criminal law to be broadly adequate.

Certainly rushing to legislate in the wake of a terrorist atrocity is often a mistake. It may be a well-intentioned mistake, designed to make us safer, but it would be better to reflect on the long-term wisdom of what may look immediately appealing. Since 9/11 there has been a slew of counter-terrorist legislation, some of it helpful, some of it justified as exceptional, partly because of the

'War on Terror' language. Quite rightly it has been scrutinised by parliament and the courts and some of it amended. Laws which involve reducing people's rights can themselves frighten the public. 'Should I be afraid,' the citizen asks, 'if the government feels these measures are necessary?'

What terrorism does is frighten us through its random effect and deter us from behaving normally. But we compound the problem of terrorism if we use it as a reason to erode the freedom of us all. That is why I spoke out against the proposal to detain terrorists without charge for up to forty-two days (ninety had been originally proposed). We were to give up something of value, in effect the principle of *habeas corpus*, and for what? Some greater spurious security? We must recognise the limits of what any government can do and be deeply cautious of anything that leads to security being seen as the opposite of liberty rather than essential to it. Governments should aim to limit and reduce the threat of terrorism, encourage its causes to be recognised and addressed, protect what it can, and be ready to react with calm when it happens, reasserting our belief in our freedoms and the rule of law.

And, as I hope I have made clear in this chapter, governments need to practice a foreign policy that, while acknowledging the world as it is, tries to secure freedom for others and to pursue a domestic policy that protects the liberties we value and which the terrorist tries to destroy.

4

The Nature of Intelligence

As I mentioned in chapter two, intelligence is the acquisition of information that is deliberately intended to be concealed. Such information should have no special value because it has been collected covertly. Its sources need to be validated, it needs to be carefully and objectively analysed and a cool assessment reached of it, involving a spectrum of expertise. It rarely offers completeness or certainty. And it needs context from other material, such as diplomatic reporting and open sources. Even with the help of context, and corroboration from other sources, intelligence can mislead. Indeed, sometimes it is intended for that purpose. It is important that those who read intelligence are not seduced by its attractions into attaching too great a significance to it. The excitement which is sometimes engendered about how it was obtained risks colouring its importance. Overt information may be more important than secret intelligence.

This may sound as if I am dumbing down the collection of intelligence and its value. I am not. It has been of major strategic importance; it has saved lives in peacetime; it has contributed to success in wartime. And, at a tactical level, the small bits which are collected help form a picture; the telephone numbers, the photographs, the association of individuals and their behaviour can all be of vital importance. But all must be judged impartially, then checked and checked again. Readers of finished, assessed reports need to be educated. New ministers and others who become readers of intelligence for the first time should approach it with healthy scepticism and questioning. The security and intelligence agencies want thoughtful, balanced and critical readers of their material, with independent judgement.

Intelligence reports always keep intelligence that has been obtained strictly separate from any comment on it, or interpretation which the originator may suggest. Feedback to those who have produced the report is important if a rich picture is to be developed.

Some other points need to be stressed. Firstly, intelligence is vulnerable. Individuals supplying it can be exposed, interrogated and killed. Our duty is to protect them. Operations can be compromised, techniques blown, ciphers changed. The targets of intelligence learn and improve their own techniques to conceal their actions from the authorities. Pleading for full public scrutiny of the techniques used potentially jeopardises those techniques. Much intelligence comes from technologies whose effectiveness, if exposed, can be countered by skilled opponents. Even more importantly, we have a high moral duty to protect human sources who risk their lives. They are also entitled to the first human right listed in the European

Convention on Human Rights, the right to life. Sources, as all journalists understand, although when it comes to intelligence sources they may pretend not to, need to be protected. Otherwise there will soon be none. That means that there can be no coercion to share intelligence, for example with foreign services. For the same reason its use in open courts needs to be carefully handled. Even if the source is not directly revealed, deductions may be made which are dangerous. In principle the Service wants to share and wishes to contribute to successful prosecutions. Intelligence is not collected, with difficulty and expense, for its own sake; there is no point. Intelligence needs to get to the right places and be used. The Service needs to develop and act on intelligence for the safety of all UK citizens and, in many cases, citizens of other countries. While prosecutions are the best outcome of counter-terrorist operations, we cannot ignore that there are real tensions here.

In the UK and elsewhere, intelligence is not only used to help track down and disrupt terrorists and others who threaten our security. It is also used to reduce the risks of terrorism more generally. Intelligence supports wider policies and action to make it more difficult for terrorists to succeed. That may involve increasing protection at key sites or on key systems to reduce their vulnerability to attack. Efforts are made to identify, map and strengthen the protection of those parts of our national infrastructure whose loss would be very damaging, and to focus resources on them.

The first challenge for intelligence staff is to find those who would cause us harm, among both the UK's population and the hundreds of thousands who visit, and to collect intelligence on them. The actions of all our citizens, or indeed citizens from elsewhere, cannot be anticipated or prevented. As my successor Jonathan Evans has said, you can know of an individual without knowing what he will do; and you can't anyway know everybody nor, and this is important, do you wish to. The next stage is to decide what action to take in response to intelligence. Who are merely talking big and who have real ambitions? Who have genuine aspirations to commit terrorism, but lack the know-how or materials? Who are the skilled and trained ones, who the amateurs? Where should the Security Service and the police focus their resources, which are always finite? Difficult choices have to be made.

And of course, all that the Service does must be done strictly within the law, the Security Service Act (1989), the Intelligence Services Act (1994) and the Regulation of Investigatory Powers Act (2000). When I joined the Service there was no law governing our work and our operations. This was a serious deficiency. I believe strongly in the rule of law. I abhor torture or the threat of it. I come from a family of lawyers and nearly studied law at university. Incidentally, my own father, Attorney General at the time of Suez, warned the British Government then that its attack on Egypt was illegal in international law. I believe that without law we are defenceless.

As well as the law, I believe in fairness and justice and not even a lawyer would claim that these always run in tandem. I do not believe that the law always gets it right. I do not believe that the Security Service always gets it right. It works in a tricky and complex environment, not only with expectations, rightly, that it should operate to the highest standards, but, as I have mentioned, with unreasonable expectations of 100 per cent prescience. Intelligence work of course raises moral and ethical issues and is not alone in doing so. Because the Service's work affects peoples' lives, freedom and privacy, it is critical to ensure that what is done is fully justified, legal, proportionate and impartial. And in that work the support is needed not only of the government of the day and, if at all possible, the opposition parties, but also of the public from whom recruits are drawn, who support operations and who supply information in confidence.

There is a genuine difficulty about communicating the level of threat. If you say nothing, the public are not alert to the dangers. If you say too much, alarm can be created. A balance has to be struck between communicating the danger so explicitly that sources are put at risk and allowing the public to remain in ignorance. And, of course, some threats fail to materialise for a range of reasons. There are those, the sceptical observers I wish the readers of intelligence to be, who believe that governments hype threats for their own purposes to ensure legislation proceeds through parliament. What the Service tries to do through its website (www.mi5.gov.uk) is to provide a cool description of the current threat level as assessed by the cross-departmental Joint Terrorist Analysis Centre whose judgements are reached, as a matter of principal, without political input.

The Service today has to deal with countries, some of which have little law, little democratic accountability, and none of the safeguards of legislation like the Police and Criminal Evidence Act. Dealing with such countries raises troubling issues. When I was Director General I discussed this dilemma with the head of Amnesty who had come to give a lecture to staff at my invitation. She thought that we should not have international relations with any foreign service which operated to moral and legal standards different to our own. The central problem of her position, which I respect, is that the global nature of terrorism requires a global response. We need intelligence from outside the UK if we are to protect our citizens from at least some of the threats we face in the twenty-first century. Many of the terrorist plots uncovered in the UK have had overseas links. In collecting intelligence relating to these events the Service must make careful judgements, paying close attention to the law and be fully accountable to the law, to ministers and through them to parliament.

We cannot always anticipate the threats that we may face, although the National Security Strategy, first drawn up by the Labour Government in 2008 and rewritten by the Coalition Government in 2010, is a welcome attempt to articulate a broad range of threats, those we know of, those we perceive as possible, and those we imagine. There is argument about its contents and its value. In view of the global economic crisis, should it refer to the risks of irresponsible capitalism? In view of the 2011 riots, should it not include a reference to civil disorder? It is healthy that what constitutes national security and what the state should do about it are debated.

In this book, I have discussed intelligence from the standpoint of my time in office. I would like to end with a cautious glance ahead. I predict that terrorism will continue to be a powerful tool in the hands of groups, and perhaps, again, of states. New groups will emerge, fuelled by the problems of the world, and their followers will learn and adapt. At some stage there will be a chemical, bacteriological or radioactive terrorist attack. Espionage, including commercial espionage, will continue to thrive. More states will acquire nuclear weapons and better means of delivering them. Tension will persist between the networked world and the need to protect some secrets. Cyber attacks, to extract information, to corrupt data or to deny service, will proliferate. Other world problems, such as climate change, energy, water supplies, pandemics and failed states all are likely to have associated security issues which may require the illumination of covert intelligence. The scrutiny of the security and intelligence agencies will evolve and it is right that it should. But, given that intelligence to counter these threats will still be needed, that scrutiny will never be able to be transparent. For to secure freedom, within a democracy and within the law, some secrets have to remain.

Acknowledgements

The Reith Lectures, which form the basis of this short book, owed much to constructive criticism from the Radio 4 team, Nicola Meyrick, Mark Savage and Jim Frank, from former colleagues in the Security Service and from family and friends.

Profile Books, which has a tradition of publishing Reith Lectures, proposed that they publish mine. My thanks to my editor at Profile, Ned Pennant-Rea, for his help with the text.

Other Reith Lectures
available from Profile Books

From Here to Infinity:
Scientific Horizons

Martin Rees

A succinct exploration of the place of science in the twenty-first century from one of the world's greatest scientists, and winner of the Templeton Prize 2011.

'A British scientist whose work has touched on the greatest questions in physics, from the nature of the Big Bang to the size of physical reality' *Guardian*

'Pithy explanation of the role of science in the global economy' *The Times*

'An absorbing summary of the state of science today' *BBC Focus*

The BBC Radio 4 Reith Lectures were given in 2010 by the Astronomer Royal, Professor Martin Rees. In this expanded version of the Lectures Rees shows how important science will be to the global economies of the twenty-first century, to solving some of our apparently intractable problems and to understanding the risks that the world faces.

ISBN: 978 1 84668 503 3
eISBN: 978 1 84765 750 3

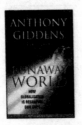

Runaway World: How Globalisation is Reshaping our Lives

Anthony Giddens

The definitive account of how the global village has shaped all our lives.

'This little book is full of insights about who we are and where we are going' *Financial Times*

Based on the highly influential BBC Reith Lecture series on globalisation delivered in 1999 by Anthony Giddens. Now updated with a new chapter addressing the post-9/11 global landscape, this book remains the intellectual benchmark on how globalisation is changing our lives. The changes are explored in five main chapters: Globalisation, Risk, Tradition, Family and Democracy.

ISBN: 978 1 86197 429 7

eISBN: 978 1 84765 103 7

The Emerging Mind

Vilayanur Ramachandran

A scintillating introduction to the latest thinking on the brain and the mind by the world's leading expert.

'An intriguing journey into the depths of the human mind'
How it Works

Professor Vilayanur Ramachandran, called 'the Marco Polo of science' by Richard Dawkins, reveals how neuroscience can begin to unlock the key to the self, based on his 2003 Reith Lectures. Our knowledge of the brain has progressed so rapidly that it will change the way we think of ourselves as human beings. This is a revolution which will have impact on all our lives. Neuroscientists are gathering new empirical evidence about consciousness and human nature; they are picking up where the great earlier thinkers like Freud, Darwin, Charcot and others began, giving substance to some of the grand statements and intuitive leaps made in the nineteenth and early twentieth century about the nature of the self.

ISBN: 978 1 86197 303 0